THE LIFE THAT WORSHIPS

WORSHIP IS THE OUTPOURING OF A SOUL AT REST

WILLIE A. BROWNING

The Life That Worships

Artwork by Joseph Weston aka *Adobe Weston*

ISBN: 9798670307369

© 2020 His Presence Church aka Willie A. Browning Publications

Willie A. Browning Publications

P.O. Box 1465

Stockbridge Ga, 30281

404-552-3088

First Words

Worship is more than a few songs on Sunday morning. Worship is a lifestyle that includes what we say but is not limited to it. It is both deliberate and involuntary. It is our response for his goodness and the seed sown for the same.

We are at the crossroads of worship. The signs read worship to please men, self, or God. We have been here before. A place where He calls for a lifestyle of devotion that transcends one day of the week. A place of love expressed, and strength received.

Mark 7:6-7 He answered and said unto them, well hath Esaias prophesied of you hypocrites, as it is written, this people honoureth me with their lips, but their heart is far from me. Howbeit in vain do they worship me, teaching for doctrines the commandments of men. We have determined this will not be our measure of inadequacy as worshipers. We are determined to honor the reason for our being which is fellowship and love.

When all is said and done, he will receive us graciously when we take these words to Him because they are filled with love and devotion. The life that worships is the life that depends entirely upon him. This life acknowledges him at every turn. It begins with our personal devotion, which is not a time for pretense but of transparency.

I John 1:7 But if we walk in the light, as he is in the light, we have fellowship one with another. (*The word light can mean to make one's thoughts known*). You see our fellowship or (worship) is dependent upon truthfulness and transparency.

This is not a revelation filled with praise and worship definitions others have done well in teaching us those. This revelation is an encouragement to return or remain (whatever your case) to our call. What is our call you ask?

My answer is Revelation 4:11 Thou art worthy, O Lord, to receive glory and honor and power: for thou hast created all things, and for thy pleasure they are and were created. My answer is 1Corinthians 1:9 God is faithful, by whom ye were called unto the fellowship of his Son Jesus Christ our Lord.

Why am I here?

Men and women all over the world have sought the answer to this question. They believed if they could answer it, it would lead to success and fulfillment. It (*their desire for the answer*) has given birth to every false religion regardless of how refined it is. Fellowship and love are the reasons for the creation of man and fellowship and love are the reasons for redemption. Not service but fellowship. God purposed a family. He wanted someone to love and fellowship with on his level. Angels were inadequate it is unlawful for them to exercise their wills; they are told what to do.

Psalm 8:3-5 When I consider thy heavens, the work of thy fingers, the moon and the stars, which thou hast ordained. What is man, that thou art mindful of him? And the son of man, that thou visitest him? For thou hast made him a little lower than the angels or the Godhead (*that Hebrew word angels is Elohim and is referring to the Godhead*) and hast crowned him with glory and honor.

God made man as close to himself as he could and gave him the gift of choice. One Hebraist writes God made man a shade lower than himself. This is the Fatherhood of God. His desire to give of himself and to express his love has given way to the creation of man. After all what good is it to be omnipotent, and omniscient if it cannot be shared with someone you love?

Ephesians 1:5-6 Having predestinated us unto the adoption of children by Jesus Christ to himself, according to the good pleasure of his will, To the praise of the glory of his grace, wherein he hath made us accepted in the beloved. We are accepted because love is the foundation for everything the Father does, and faith filled words is the way he does it. John 3:16 For God so loved the world, that he gave his only begotten Son. Love was his motivation. Paul said in 2 Corinthians 5:14 For the love of Christ constraineth us (it means to be pressed in spirit) Paul is saying love is the reason we do what we do. This is the life that worships. This life is devoted to him. Now when you stand and worship corporately you are unashamed before men and fearless before the enemy. You are not self-conscious but God inside me conscious.

Willie Browning

CONTENTS

Chapter 1

THE RESPONSIBILITIES OF THE WORSHIPER

Responsibility #1 Is to Worship

We are worshipers by nature we are always worshiping someone or something. God made us this way. Hebrews 10:1-2 For the law having a shadow of good things to come, and not the very image of the things, can never with those sacrifices which they offered year by year continually make the comers thereunto perfect. For then would they not have ceased to be offered? Because that the worshippers once purged should have had no more conscience of sins.

God created this desire and ability inside us. So, do not limit your view of worship to mean singing songs in a church service. Your lifestyle should be worship to the Father. Romans 12:1 I beseech you therefore, brethren, by the mercies of God, that ye present your bodies a living sacrifice, holy, acceptable unto God, which is your reasonable service. The Amplified Bible reads which is your reasonable (rational, intelligent) service and spiritual worship. You would think the average believer knows this but sadly some do not.

I believe our concentration has been more to the entertainment of men to the point we have missed our primary calling. For example, I am not against musical competitions I'm sure they serve their purpose, but how do you judge love, faithfulness, and loyalty merely by how someone sings or plays? You cannot. Remember 1Samuel 16:7 *The Message Translation* God told Samuel, "Looks aren't everything. Don't be impressed with his looks and stature. I've already eliminated him. God judges persons differently than humans do. Men and women look at the face; God looks into the heart.

The Life That Worships

2Corinthians 10:12 *The Message Translation*- We're not, understand, putting ourselves in a league with those who boast that they're our superiors. We wouldn't dare do that. But in all this comparing and grading and competing, they quite miss the point.

I think sometimes we miss the point. This is not a criticism but an observation. 1 Corinthians 1:9 God is faithful, by whom ye were called unto the fellowship of his Son Jesus Christ our Lord. What would happen to our worship if our primary goal were the pleasing of the Father and not the praise of men? I believe it would cut down most of the competitiveness' that people engage in to receive the honor that comes from men. It freed me up years ago when I found out I am a gift to the body of Christ and the world, a gift that should be received by faith. My ability to do whatever I do is not as great as some, and greater than others, big gift, small gift all I am is a gift. And the thanks that should be offered for the gift should go to the giver, God the Father.

Ephesians 1:6 To the praise of the glory of his grace, wherein he hath made us accepted in the beloved. We are accepted because of what Jesus did not because of what we do. When we pray, fast, study and confess His Word it is because we are accepted and not to be accepted by Him.

We must spend time with Him. not out of compulsion but out of our desire for Him. Luke 10:41-42 And Jesus answered and said unto her, Martha, Martha, thou art careful and troubled about many things: But one thing is needful: and Mary hath chosen that good part, which shall not be taken away from her. The Lord said one thing is needful, that needful thing is fellowship with Him.

I have learned that truth over the years sometimes the easy way, sometimes the hard way. But I have learned my fellowship with Him is paramount. I remember years ago in the late seventies I went on a fast and the same day I played basketball I almost passed out. I did not understand then that if you are going to fast you should spend time with the Father as much as you can and limit your activity as much as you can. I reduced my fast to merely not eating food obviously there was truly little spiritual benefit. That is what happens on a Sunday morning people are part of a worship team and Jesus is the last person on their mind. And they do what I did those years ago they reduced their ministry to their ability to sing or play and they get the same results I got truly little if any anointing at all. As Kingdom musicians and singers, we not only impart what we do and say we impart who we are.

We will spend our time somewhere, it might be the doctor's office or lawyer's office or the principal's office at the children's school, why not spend that time with Him.

Responsibility #2

To Protect the Anointing (call)

Ephesians 4:1 I therefore, the prisoner of the Lord, beseech you that ye walk worthy of the vocation wherewith ye are called. This vocation of which Paul speaks is all encompassing. He speaks of salvation, husband and wife relationships, parent and child, Christian to Christian and so on. Paul writes endeavoring to keep the unity of the Spirit. Do not allow anything or anyone to come between your fellowship with Him and others.

1Corinthians 1:9-10 God is faithful, by whom ye were called unto the fellowship of his Son Jesus Christ our Lord. Now I beseech you, brethren, by the name of our Lord Jesus Christ, that ye all speak the same thing, and that there be no divisions among you; but that ye be perfectly joined together in the same mind and in the same judgment.

Our primary calling is to him, to the body of Christ, and then to the world. This should be the same protocol as it relates to our Worship. We enter His gates, then His courts, then His presence.

1Corinthians 15:33 Be not deceived evil communications corrupt good manners. *NIV Translation*-Do not be misled bad company corrupts good character.

Let us mind our intake remember Proverbs 4:23 Keep or (guard) thy heart with all diligence; for out of it are the issues of life. What we see hear and who we associate with enhances or hinders our fellowship with him. Paul writes come out from among them and be separate. Because a leaven leavens the whole lump. People protect their homes, families, and possessions, let us protect our time with Him.

The Life That Worships

David Sees Bathsheba Bathing

2Samuel 11:2 And it came to pass in an eveningtide, that David arose from off his bed, and walked upon the roof of the king's house: and from the roof he saw a woman washing herself; and the woman *was* very beautiful to look upon.

Protecting the fellowship, we have with Him and the anointing we have from Him is our responsibility. What we look at today could be seed sown for a harvest two weeks from now good or bad.

2Samuel 11:3-4 And David sent and enquired after the woman. And *one* said, *Is* not this Bathsheba, the daughter of Eliam, the wife of Uriah the Hittite? And David sent messengers, and took her; and she came in unto him, and he lay with her; for she was purified from her uncleanness: and she returned unto her house.

James 1:13-15 Let no man say when he is tempted, I am tempted of God: for God cannot be tempted with evil, neither tempteth he any man: But every man is tempted, when he is drawn away of his own lust, and enticed. Then when lust hath conceived, it bringeth forth sin: and sin, when it is finished, bringeth forth death.

The seed sown gets in through our senses, what we see what we hear and so on. Sometimes a thought that goes unchecked is all the enemy needs to trick us. 2Corinthians 10:5 Casting down imaginations, and every high thing that exalteth itself against the knowledge of God and bringing into captivity every thought to the obedience of Christ.

Responsibility #3

To be a faithful steward of the mystery of Worship

1Corinthians 4:1-2 Let a man so account of us, as of the ministers of Christ, and stewards of the mysteries of God. Moreover it is required in stewards, that a man be found faithful. (I have taken this out of context to apply it to Worship).

A steward is one who rules a house a superior servant responsible for other servants, the direction of other servants and the care of children underage.

The Responsibilities Of The Worshiper

In Contrast

A hireling is a wage worker a hired servant one who has no real interest in his duty and one who is unfaithful in the discharge of it. All he wants is the money or recognition that comes with the call.

2Timothy 2; 1-4 Thou therefore, my son, be strong in the grace that is in Christ Jesus. And the things that thou hast heard of me among many witnesses, the same commit thou to faithful men, who shall be able to teach others also.

A premium has been placed on faithfulness over ability. Ability is important but not as important as being able to be counted on.

Proverbs 20:6 Most men will proclaim everyone his own goodness: but a faithful man who can find? It does not matter how well you do what you do if you're not in place when you should be. I am speaking to Kingdom Worshipers and Musicians.

New Living Translation-Many will say they are loyal friends, but who can find one who is truly reliable?

It has been said that when you do not know the reason for a thing, abuse is inevitable. Having stated that, being faithful to dig in the word and find your place, your gift and then spend years developing that same gift is God's will for you.

To those called as Kingdom Musicians this should be your quest. Do not stop with natural abilities, find in the word how through your playing and singing people can receive healing and how marriages can be restored. Do not be satisfied until evil spirits are driven out as with David and Saul. Our goal is to move over into the supernatural with our natural abilities. Take David as an example. How much concentration effort and discipline he must have had to develop a trust in the Father the way he did. 1Samuel 17:33-37- And Saul said to David, Thou art not able to go against this Philistine to fight with him: for thou art but a youth, and he a man of war from his youth. And David said unto Saul, Thy servant kept his father's sheep, and there came a lion, and a bear, and took a lamb out of the flock: And I went out after him, and smote him, and delivered it out of his mouth: and when he arose against me, I caught him by his beard, and smote him, and slew him. Thy servant slew both the lion and the bear: and this uncircumcised Philistine shall be as one of them, seeing he hath defied the armies of the living God. David said moreover, The Lord that delivered me out of the paw of the lion, and out of the paw of the bear, he will deliver me out of the hand of this Philistine. And Saul said unto David, Go, and the Lord be with thee.

Let us parallel this event with our Sunday morning services. David's attitude towards Goliath was predetermined. It had already been developed before he even met Goliath. It should be the same way with us. We do not drum up the anointing because we have an audience, what we have on Sunday is an overflow of the way we live every day.

Responsibility #4

You Are Not for Hire You Are for Call

Leaders have created an unhealthy paradigm. In our attempt to grow ministry we have been more concerned with talent than the development of people. We have seen people as tools to help us achieve our personal goals instead of assets of the Kingdom.

Be A Servant Leader

Mark 9:33-35 And he came to Capernaum and being in the house he asked them, What was it that ye disputed among yourselves by the way? But they held their peace for by the way they had disputed among themselves, who should be the greatest. And he sat down, and called the twelve, and saith unto them, if any man desires to be first, the same shall be last of all, and servant of all.

When leaders do not require spiritual commitment from those who operate in music ministry it is a revelation of ignorance or questionable motives. Sometimes especially with smaller ministries Pastors feel they must compromise because of the need, but they do not. Sometimes if you compromise to get you have to compromise to keep. This is not a job or career it is a call so you cannot be bought. I sing and preach If I get paid or not. The Father has graced me,

The Responsibilities Of The Worshiper

I do what I do with Him and it is up to Him to meet every need. *Easy To Read Version*-1Corinthians 9:7 No one ever plants a vineyard without eating some of the grapes himself. No one takes care of a flock of sheep without drinking some of the milk himself.

The Dreaded I Will Play If You Pay Mentality

This will be the attitude when people consider their gifts a career instead of a calling. Money is important, in the old Testament the Levitical singers lived in their own community apart from the people.

Find your place in the body of Christ to grow-Psalms 92:12-14-The righteous shall flourish like the palm tree: he shall grow like a cedar in Lebanon. Those that be planted in the house of the LORD shall flourish in the courts of our God. They shall still bring forth fruit in old age; they shall be fat and flourishing.

Because It Is Your Calling Not Your Career

Value the gift Genesis25:34 Then Jacob gave Esau bread and pottage of lentiles; and he did eat and drink, and rose up, and went his way thus Esau despised his birthright. A Hireling is a wage worker a hired servant one who has no real interest in his duty and one who is unfaithful in the discharge of it. All he wants is the money or recognition that comes with the call.

To Leaders in The Body of Christ Ask Yourselves About Those Under Your Care

Do they have an appetite for prayer? Luke 18:1

Do they have an appetite for the word? Job 23:12

Are they consistent with church attendance? Heb 10;25

Are they submitted to delegated authority? Heb 13:17

Are they concerned with anything else other than music?

Are they givers?

The Life That Worships

Whenever there was cleansing and revival it was accompanied by the restoration of worship 2Chronicles 29:25-27

Nehemiah 11:22-23 a portion for the singers

Responsibility #5

Worship in the beauty of Holiness

No area is more crucial to the manifestation of God's glory than holiness. Without a revelation of it, all we have are gifts without substance and form without power. If you are a Christian especially a Kingdom musician can we depend on the anointing upon your life weekend week out to help us in our worship to Him, or are we left to rely solely on your ability?

2Kings 3:14-15 And Elisha said, As the LORD of hosts liveth, before whom I stand, surely, were it not that I regard the presence of Jehoshaphat the king of Judah, I would not look toward thee, nor see thee. But now bring me a minstrel. And it came to pass, when the minstrel played, that the hand of the LORD came upon him.

Back in the early 1980s the Lord helped me to see that as a worship leader I am not the one, I am just making way for the one I am just like John the Baptist. But he helped me to see how important my ministry is to the Man and Woman of God. In 1Corinthians 12:28 Paul calls it the helps ministry.

Can we release his presence at will by faith? Or are we totally dependent upon His discretion? Do we have a part to play? Does my relationship with my wife affect the worship on Sunday morning? Matthew 18:20 Psalms 22:3 We must set a standard and be vigilant to guard it, we must protect our ministries and keep them pure (*This is worshipping in the beauty of holiness or praising Him for His beauty which is holiness*)

The Big Three

1Jn 2:1516 Love not the world, neither the things *that are* in the world. If any man love the world, the love of the Father is not in him. For all that *is* in the world, the lust of the flesh, and the lust of the eyes, and the pride of life, is not of the Father, but is of the world.

The Responsibilities Of The Worshiper

All That Is In The World

The lust of the eyes: covetousness a cruel and grasping lover of money envious wanting what belongs to another Psalms 119:36 Rivers of waters run down mine eyes, because they keep not thy law.

The pride of life: Proverbs 16:18-19 Pride *goeth* before destruction, and an haughty spirit before a fall. Better *it is to be* of an humble spirit with the lowly, than to divide the spoil with the proud.

There are different kinds of pride Romans 12:3 1Peter 5:6-7

1Chronicles 16:27-29-Glory and honour *are* in his presence; strength and gladness *are* in his place. Give unto the LORD, ye kindreds of the people, give unto the LORD glory and strength. Give unto the LORD the glory due unto his name: bring an offering and come before him worship the LORD in the beauty of holiness. We decide to live right, no excuses.

What Kind of Vessel Are You?

2Timothy 2:20-21 But in a great house there are not only vessels of gold and of silver, but also of wood and of earth; and some to honor, and some to dishonor. If a man therefore purges himself from these, he shall be a vessel unto honor, sanctified, and meet for the master's use, and prepared unto every good work. Can you see the correlation between gold silver and honor versus wood earth and dishonor? Do you understand what is important to him? I know you do.

1Corinthians 9:24-27-Know ye not that they which run in a race run all, but one receiveth the prize? So run, that ye may obtain. And every man that strives for the mastery is temperate in all things. Now they do it to obtain a corruptible crown; but we an incorruptible. I therefore so run, not as uncertainly so fight I, not as one that beateth the air: But I keep under my body, and bring it into subjection: lest that by any means, when I have preached to others, I myself should be a castaway.

More Scriptures To Study

2Chronicles 20:21 Praising Him for His beauty which is Holiness

The Life That Worships

Psalms 29:2

Psalms 96:4-9

Psalms 24:3

Chapter 2

WHAT IS WORSHIP?

The character of our worship is determined by the quality of our hearts. 1Samuel 16:7 But the LORD said unto Samuel, Look not on his countenance, or on the height of his stature; because I have refused him for the LORD seeth not as man seeth; for man looketh on the outward appearance, but the LORD looketh on the heart.

Our worship should be from the inside out. This is the point I made earlier about musical competitions; man looks on the outer God looks at the heart.

The quality of our worship is determined by our estimation of him. Matthew 26:6-13 Now when Jesus was in Bethany, in the house of Simon the leper, There came unto him a woman having an alabaster box of very precious ointment, and poured it on his head, as he sat at meat. But when his disciples saw it, they had indignation, saying, to what purpose is this waste? For this ointment might have been sold for much and given to the poor. When Jesus understood it, he said unto them, why trouble ye the woman? For she hath wrought a good work upon me. For ye have the poor always with you; but me ye have not always. For in that she hath poured this ointment on my body, she did it for my burial. Verily I say unto you, wheresoever this gospel shall be preached in the whole world, there shall also this, that this woman hath done, be told for a memorial of her.

The quality of our worship is determined by our estimation of Him, what a powerful truth to meditate on. Understanding this will solve the sin problem in our lives it will cause us to be bold fearless and sure because He has become our sufficiency.

To what purpose is this waste? What a strange question to ask the Son of God. What ignorance shown in the presence of Deity. Our preparation, sacrifice, time and even money are not to be compared to God. Time spent in prayer, all that we can do or give are not to be compared to Him. The quality of our worship is determined by our estimation of him. The disciples asked to what purpose is this waste. Jesus said leave her alone for she has wrought a good work upon me. Our worship is a good work. I was listening to a well-known Minister and he said God sent him across the world to minister to one woman. The expense is worth it the effort and time are all worth it when we do it for Him.

There were many things the apostles were not aware of at that time for those few years they walked with the man seeing the miracles experiencing His love walk and listening to His wisdom they still did not completely get it. It was only until God gave the revelation of what happened in the realm of the spirit to Paul that they could really understand. In Peter's second letter he wrote about Paul 2Peter 3:16 As also in all *his* epistles, speaking in them of these things; in which are some things hard to be understood, which they that are unlearned and unstable wrest, as *they do* also the other scriptures, unto their own destruction.

That is the way it is with worship there are levels of understanding levels of love levels of obedience. The more we understand His love for us and what He has done for us the deeper and higher our worship.

Luke 7:47 Wherefore I say unto thee, Her sins, which are many, are forgiven; for she loved much: but to whom little is forgiven, *the same* loveth little. This is what I mean by levels of worship, as you and I get a deeper level of His love and how He has forgiven us worship will continue to grow and deepen. When we realize we were not just saved from hell, but we were saved to living forever with Him and His provisions.

Worship is costly 2Samuel 24:22-25-And Araunah said unto David, Let my lord the king take and offer up what seemeth good unto him behold, here be oxen for burnt sacrifice, and threshing instruments and other instruments of the oxen for wood. All these things did Araunah, as a king, give unto the king. And Araunah said unto the king, The LORD thy God accept thee. And the king said unto Araunah, Nay; but I will surely buy it of thee at a price: neither will I offer burnt offerings unto the LORD my God of that which doth cost me nothing. So, David bought the threshing floor and the oxen for fifty shekels of silver. And David built there an altar unto the LORD, and offered burnt offerings and peace offerings. So the LORD was intreated for the land, and the plague was stayed from Israel.

This worship is costly in so many respects. It can cost you your reputation, your pride and fear. It will require honesty when ordinarily we would slip and slide to get by. Genesis 22 Abraham had no precedence for his son being raised from the dead. This is what I mean by mature, you hear from God and do what he says to do, this also is worship. Isaac represented us, the ram in the bush represented Jesus. We see Abraham giving an immediate response and his worship was costly Abraham offered his future to God. His obedience was his worship. You do not see Abraham fussing with his wife about killing her son I think it is important to note that the bible at this point did not say anything about Abraham's wife as it related to the sacrifice.

Worship is the overflow of a grateful heart. Luke 17:12-19 And as he entered into a certain village, there met him ten men that were lepers, which stood afar off: And they lifted up their voices, and said, Jesus, Master, have mercy on us. And when he saw them, he said unto them, Go show yourselves unto the priests. And it came to pass, that, as they went, they were cleansed. And one of them, when he saw that he was healed, turned back, and with a loud voice glorified God, and fell down on his face at his feet, giving him thanks: and he was a Samaritan. And Jesus answering said, were there not ten cleansed? But where are the nine? There are not found that returned to give glory to God, save this stranger. And he said unto him, Arise, go thy way: thy faith hath made thee whole.

We see obedience got the leper moving but gratitude brought him back. In addition, we see worship is a release of faith, because in thanking Jesus the Lord said your faith has made you whole. You and I know that people who are grateful for what you do say thank you.

The Life That Worships

Thanksgiving is grateful language as an act of worship, we remember what He has done for us and what He is doing now. 2Corinthians 1:9-10 But we had the sentence of death in ourselves, that we should not trust in ourselves, but in God which raiseth the dead: Who delivered us from so great a death, and doth deliver: in whom we trust that he will yet deliver *us*. We will not forget any of His benefits. We constantly remind ourselves of the benefits of being His child and so we thank Him.

Worship is the outpouring of a soul at rest. When we get into his presence, we can make adjustments that otherwise are exceedingly difficult to make. He gives us strength and takes our weakness. There are times you do not know where the money is coming from, but you rest. Perhaps you have received a report from the doctor that you do not have long to live but still you rest. Hebrews 4:11 Let us labor therefore to enter into that rest, lest any man fall after the same example of unbelief. Make every effort is what the word labor means. You are not falling apart like a two-dollar watch. Because you are resting you already have the answer.

The Message Translation Matthew 11:28-30 Are you tired? Worn out? Burned out on religion? Come to me. Get away with me and you'll recover your life. I'll show you how to take a real rest. Walk with me and work with me watch how I do it. Learn the unforced rhythms of grace. I won't lay anything heavy or ill-fitting on you. Keep company with me and you'll learn to live freely and lightly.

A soul at rest trust God this soul may not know where the help is coming from, but that soul knows it is coming. This soul has ceased from his own labor and has entered God's rest.

Worship is the occupation of the heart not with its need or blessings but with the Father himself. He is looking for someone to go beyond what he has given to centering their love on him. The old saying encourages us to seek his face and not his hand. 2Chronicles 1:10-12 Give me now wisdom and knowledge that I may go out and come in before this people: for who can judge this thy people, that is so great? And God said to Solomon, Because this was in thine heart, and thou hast not asked riches, wealth, or honor, nor the life of thine enemies, neither yet hast asked long life; but hast asked wisdom and knowledge for thyself, that thou mayest judge my people, over whom I have made thee king wisdom and knowledge is granted unto thee; and I will give thee riches, and wealth, and honour, such as none of the kings have had that have been before thee, neither shall there any after thee have the like. Can't you see it's a heart issue?

We hear from him as a result of worship Act 13:1-2 Now there were in the church that was at Antioch certain prophets and teachers; as Barnabas, and Simeon that was called Niger, and Lucius of Cyrene, and Manaen, which had been brought up with Herod the tetrarch, and Saul. As they ministered to the Lord, and fasted, the Holy Ghost said, Separate me Barnabas and Saul for the work whereunto I have called them.

Worship is living water returning to its source Ecclesiastes 1:7 All the rivers run into the sea; yet the sea *is* not full; unto the place from whence the rivers come, thither they return again.

John 4:14 But whosoever drinketh of the water that I shall give him shall never thirst; but the water that I shall give him shall be in him a well of water springing up into everlasting life. This speaks of the new birth.

John 7:38-39 He that believeth on me, as the scripture hath said, out of his belly shall flow rivers of living water. (But this spake he of the Spirit, which they that believe on him should receive: for the Holy Ghost was not yet *given;* because that Jesus was not yet glorified.) This speaks of being filled with the Holy Spirit.

Worship demands a separation from those around you and true worship will end with the blessing. By that I mean we must do it God's way regardless of the fall out. Peter said we ought to obey God instead of man. Matthew 10:34-37 Think not that I am come to send peace on earth: I came not to send peace, but a sword. For I am come to set a man at variance against his father, and the daughter against her mother, and the daughter in law against her mother in law. And a man's foes *shall be* they of his own household. He that loveth father or mother more than me is not worthy of me: and he that loveth son or daughter more than me is not worthy of me.

The Life That Worships

Worship is an act or acts of obedience Genesis 22:3-10 Hebrews 11:17 As with Abraham God provided the lamb (worship) we offer to him; we provide a heart filled with love and faith. True worship is attending upon the Lord without distractions.

Chapter #3

THE FORCE OF SOUND

Worshipers by nature

As I have stated whenever I am afforded an opportunity to teach on Praise and Worship, I let people know that we are worshippers by nature. We are always worshiping someone or something because worship is innate.

Hebrews 10:1-2-For the law having a shadow of good things to come, and not the very image of the things, can never with those sacrifices which they offered year by year continually make the comers thereunto perfect. For then would they not have ceased to be offered? Because that the worshippers once purged should have had no more conscience of sins.

There are two Spiritual Overlords, God and Satan, and our worship is always directed towards one or the other. This truth must be understood. For example, James 3:11 Does a fountain send forth at the same place sweet water and bitter? 1John 3:10 In this the children of God are manifest, and the children of the devil: whosoever doeth not righteousness is not of God, neither he that loveth not his brother. What we call humanism is really man worshiping the devil because he is not his own Lord. Sometimes that worship is born out of ignorance, but it is still satanic worship non the less.

Hosea 14:1-2 O Israel, return unto the LORD thy God for thou hast fallen by thine iniquity. Take with you words, and turn to the LORD say unto him, Take away all iniquity, and receive us graciously so will we render the calves or (praise) of our lips.

The Life That Worships

God is love but he creates everything with faith filled words. Jesus said my words are spirit and they are life. How can we use words in our worship to not only bless the Lord, but as an aid in the exercising of victory over the enemy? Psalms 8:2 Out of the mouth of babes and sucklings hast thou ordained strength or (praise) because of thine enemies, that thou mightest still the enemy and the avenger. Do you see that? Even from babes and suckling's we know how to praise God because it is innate. The word still means to be inactive; it means to silence. We need a revelation that while music ministry has an entertaining element to it, the greatest value is what happens in the realm of the Spirit. Acts 16:25-26 And at midnight Paul and Silas prayed, and sang praises unto God: and the prisoners heard them. And suddenly there was a great earthquake, so that the foundations of the prison were shaken and immediately all the doors were opened, and every one's bands were loosed. Obviously, someone was behind the words these men were singing. We know the source because we know the outcome.

Offering Faith and Love filled Words

1 Peter 2:1-5 Wherefore laying aside all malice, and all guile, and hypocrisies, and envies, and all evil speaking, As newborn babies, desire the sincere milk of the word, that ye may grow thereby If so be ye have tasted that the Lord is gracious. To whom coming, as unto a living stone, disallowed indeed of men, but chosen of God, and precious, Ye also, as lively stones, are built up a spiritual house, an holy priesthood to offer up spiritual sacrifices, acceptable to God by Jesus Christ.

We are a holy priesthood, and the sacrifices we offer are the sacrifices of praise (Hebrews 13:15). Let me give it the way the Lord gave it to me. We belong to a *physically pure, morally blameless, Kingly in nature, Priestly fraternity.* This is the office we stand in. Many think the sacrifice of praise is praising God when you do not feel like it. It is not; it is our ministry as New Testament priest.

1 Pet 2:9 But ye are a chosen generation, a royal priesthood, an holy nation, a peculiar people; that ye should show forth the praises of him who hath called you out of darkness into his marvelous light. You can see vertical and horizontal praise. You can see our ministry to him and ministry for him

The Force Of Sound

Words

When we understand the importance of words and that they are spiritual forces, we begin to understand how our words affect the world of the spirit. Jesus said the words that I speak are spirit and they are life. He also said by our words we are justified or condemned. The importance of words in praise must not be overlooked. When we fellowship with him and offer these faith and love filled words, he receives them gladly. Remember Hosea 14:1-2 O Israel, return unto the LORD thy God for thou hast fallen by thine iniquity. Take with you words and turn to the LORD say unto him, Take away all iniquity, and receive us graciously so will we render the calves (or praise) of our lips.

Words are especially important to him and should be to us. He inhabits them. He refuses to do without them. He cannot and will not stay away from words or sounds made in his honor. But these same words when directed to-wards the enemy will win the victory for us every time. Think about it, on one hand he makes his home in our words. But on the other hand, we paralyze the enemy with the same words. Words are spiritual forces that can penetrate even the darkest situation. Words are also spiritual containers that can carry faith or fear, love or hate. It all depends on what your heart is filled with.

Luke 6:45-A good man out of the good treasure of his heart bringeth forth that which is good; and an evil man out of the evil treasure of his heart bringeth forth that which is evil for of the abundance of the heart his mouth speaketh.

Praise is what we are in the way it is what we do. It is a revelation of what is on the inside. It flows from us in good times and stressful times we cannot help it. Words are forever coming out of our mouths either glorifying God or Satan.

He lives in faith filled words

Psalm 22:2-3-But thou art holy, O thou that inhabitest the praises of Israel. He has made our words his home. Make him feel welcome there as you minister to him continually. Many are asking for money and deliverance, which are both his will. But what would happen if we asked for a revelation of the power of faith filled words? What would happen to our churches, our homes, and lives if we mastered this? I believe this knowledge would lift us and carry us to another level. The Father lives in our words and where he lives there is liberty. Jesus

25

knew the power of words. He wanted to leave that knowledge with the world.

Philippians 4:6 Be careful for nothing; but in everything by prayer and supplication with thanksgiving let your requests be made known unto God. The connection is this when you pray in faith you believe that you receive. When you have what you desire you thank God for it. Not only that, but your praise empowers your words. Or better yet your praise carries your words to the place they ordinarily would not be able to go on their own.

He desires them

John 4:23 But the hour cometh, and now is, when the true worshippers shall worship the Father in spirit and in truth: for the Father seeketh such to worship him. Not only does he desire faith and love filled words when we praise him, but he requires us to offer them in spirit and truth. Luke 17:17-18 And Jesus answering said, Were there not ten cleansed? But where are the nine? There are not found that returned to give glory to God, save this stranger.

I learned in the early days of my walk with him that fellowship is important to him and should be to us. Truthfully, every victory or defeat can be traced to our fellowship with him or lack thereof. Remember John:15 abide in me and my words in you for without me you can do nothing.

Thanksgiving and Praise your spiritual protocol

Thanksgiving and Praise are faith enhancers. These twins can keep your faith up there when you are tempted to throw in the towel. They will keep you energized through the tough times. Romans 4:19-20 And being not weak in faith, he considered not his own body now dead, when he was about an hundred years old, neither yet the deadness of Sarah's womb He staggered not at the promise of God through unbelief; but was strong in faith, giving glory to God. You can see how his faith was affected by his praise. The word glory means to give honor that results from a good opinion, it means to praise.

When we go to the Father we should as Psalms 100 states enter into his gates with thanksgiving and into his courts with praise. This is our Worship Protocol. Psalms 100:2 come before his presence with singing. Praise, and worship, accomplish much as we come before the Father. #1. It places the emphasis where it belongs, on Him and not the problem. #2. It helps you to become he wants to help me conscious rather than I am at my wits end conscious. #3. Know that words are spiritual forces. We need that revelation deep within our hearts, that when we come to him with faith filled words, he will honor them.

Hebrews 4:16- Let us therefore come boldly unto the throne of grace, that we may obtain mercy, and find grace to help in time of need. The word boldly means with freedom of speech, all out spokenness. We come to him with a mouth filled with words. Not the problem alone, but covenant promises that cover what you face. I know from the word and from experience that singing my love to him pleases him more than any other thing I can do. Psalms 69:30-31-I will praise the name of God with a song and will magnify him with thanksgiving. This also shall please the LORD better than an ox or bullock that hath horns and hoofs. Faith pleases him Hebrews 11:6. Now I see that faith and love filled singing pleases him. According to the psalmist the sacrifice of praise pleases him more than any other sacrifice I can offer. Remember the sacrifices for the New Testament believer are words.

You can see why many prayers go unanswered. Not because He does not want to help, but because our approach has hindered him from helping. Many have come to him trying to talk him into helping. But he is already touched with the feelings of our infirmities. We should have filled our hearts with the covenant we have with him and filled our mouths with praise and thanksgiving as we approached Him. We would have had much more successful prayer lives. At some point the Body of Christ should understand this. At some point let us wake up to this, how we sound is not more important than who he is. John 5:44 How can ye believe, which receive honor one of another, and seek not the honor that cometh from God only? Sometimes our desire to entertain gets in the way. As Kingdom worshipers let us be entertaining, but let's be anointed first.

2 Chronicles 20:17-19 Ye shall not need to fight in this battle set yourselves, stand ye still, and see the salvation of the LORD with you, O Judah and Jerusalem fear not, nor be dismayed; tomorrow go out against them for the LORD will be with you. And Jehoshaphat bowed his head with his face to the ground: and all Judah and the inhabitants of Jerusalem fell before the LORD, worshipping the LORD. And the Levites, of the children of the Kohathites, and of the children of the Korhites, stood up to praise the LORD God of Israel with a loud voice on high.

The Life That Worships

You see their reaction to pressure. Jehoshaphat worshipped and the people praised. I love this because I have done it so many times. I have seen the Lord move miraculously in my life.

We are going deeper into this lifestyle of worship. Receiving applause in a church service has taken back seat to knowing how to release and cooperate with the Father's presence. I remember several times preaching funerals for families I did not know. What do you say to someone about their love one that is gone, and you have never met them? What do you do when you get a call that a love one has been taken to the hospital? You do what Jesus did. Notice in his life and ministry he always drew from the Father. He did nothing on his own and repeated only what he heard. In times of great stress, he spent time with the Father, the garden of Gethsemane is an example. When it was time to choose the disciples, he spent all night in prayer to God.

I am sure that we do not go far enough in Spiritual things. You can agree there are times we have had this fast food drive through mentality. We take vacations to rest our minds and bodies. But who ever heard of taking a week off just to spend time with God?

Hosea 6:3 Then shall we know if we follow on to know the LORD his going forth is prepared as the morning and he shall come unto us as the rain, as the latter and former rain unto the earth.

The *New International Version*- reads Let us acknowledge the Lord; let us press on to acknowledge him. As surely as the sun rises, he will appear; he will come to us like the winter rains, like the spring rains that water the earth.

Jeremiah 29:12-13 Then shall ye call upon me, and ye shall go and pray unto me, and I will hearken unto you. And ye shall seek me, and find me, when ye shall search for me with all your heart.

Philippians 3:15 Let us therefore, as many as be perfect, be thus minded and if in anything ye be otherwise minded, God shall reveal even this unto you.

This is the side of Praise and Worship we are delving into. Spending time in his presence. Receiving wisdom, knowledge, and understanding. Living this Christian life from the inside out.

You shall not need to fight

The people of God are facing insurmountable odds as far as they are concerned. Their backs are against the wall and they do not know what to do. 2Chronicles 20:3 And Jehoshaphat feared, and set himself to seek the LORD, and proclaimed a fast throughout all Judah. I thank God they had competent leadership; I thank God the King did not fall apart like a two-dollar watch. I thank God he had the revelation when my heart is overwhelmed lead me to the Rock that is higher than I. I thank God he did not turn on the TV to be entertained.

2Chronicles 20:17-19 Ye shall not need to fight in this battle set yourselves, stand ye still, and see the salvation of the LORD with you, O Judah and Jerusalem: fear not, nor be dismayed; tomorrow go out against them: for the LORD will be with you. And Jehoshaphat bowed his head with his face to the ground: and all Judah and the inhabitants of Jerusalem fell before the LORD, worshipping the LORD.

And the Levites, of the children of the Kohathites, and of the children of the Korhites, stood up to praise the LORD God of Israel with a loud voice on high.

What they said was significant to their victory

By design I have omitted a lot of Praise and Worship definitions. I have stated that others have adequately taught us those. In this revelation I want you to get the spirit behind the Hebrew and Greek words. The bible says they fell before the Lord worshipping and they stood up to praise the Lord saying, Praise the LORD; for his mercy endureth for ever. And when they began to sing and to praise, the LORD set ambushments against the children of Ammon, Moab, and mount Seir.

Obviously, there is something or someone backing the words spoken. Obviously, this level of praise and worship is different than at other time. Now the question is how we can encourage a manifestation of the Spirit like this. Is there any deliberate action or response on our part? Psalms 67:5 Let the people praise thee, O God; let all the people praise thee. Then shall the earth yield her increase; and God, even our own God, shall bless us. Prosperity was God's response to their praise. Jesus said the Father seeks worshippers to worship in spirit and in truth. You are beginning to see it now.

A manifestation of his glory

Mark 9:16-18 And he asked the scribes, What question ye with them? And one of the multitude answered and said, Master, I have brought unto thee my son, which hath a dumb spirit. And wheresoever he taketh him, he teareth him and he foameth, and gnasheth with his teeth, and pineth away: and I spake to thy disciples that they should cast him out and they could not.

Matthew 17:19-20 Then came the disciples to Jesus apart, and said, Why could not we cast him out? And Jesus said unto them, Because of your unbelief.

There is a reason we are limited to only good sounding worship services at church, and why we are so distracted in our private devotions. Because of improper priorities, and questionable motives, the disciples were more concerned about personal position than ministry deliverance.

The right way

2Chronicles 5:13-14 It came even to pass, as the trumpeters and singers were as one, to make one sound to be heard in praising and thanking the LORD and when they lifted up their voice with the trumpets and cymbals and instruments of music, and praised the LORD, saying, For he is good; for his mercy endures for ever that then the house was filled with a cloud, even the house of the LORD. So that the priests could not stand to minister by reason of the cloud for the glory of the LORD had filled the house of God.

Acts 19:16:25-26 And at midnight Paul and Silas prayed, and sang praises unto God and the prisoners heard them. And suddenly there was a great earthquake, so that the foundations of the prison were shaken and immediately all the doors were opened, and every one's bands were loosed. Dr. Kenneth Weust in his word studies point out that they had shackles around their necks and feet. Also, the prisoners not only heard but enjoyed their singing. No, they were not singing come by here my Lord or don't take your Spirit away from me. Their songs were impregnated with faith and love filled words. You know Paul was not singing a bunch of unbelief.

The Force Of Sound

There are levels of intimacy and commitment in life, and the same thing applies to our worship. The more attention we give to him in our worship (our daily lives), the more of his glory will be experienced. The more we look at him the more we look like him. 2Corinthians 3:18 But we all, with open face beholding as in a glass the glory of the Lord, are changed into the same image from glory to glory, even as by the Spirit of the Lord.

Chapter #4

HINDRANCES TO WORSHIP

God is Looking for Worshippers

In chapter 4 of the Gospel of John, Jesus told the woman at the well, "God is looking for those who will worship Him." Second Chronicles 16:9 says, For the eyes of the Lord run to and fro throughout the whole earth, to show himself strong in the behalf of them whose heart is perfect toward him. The Father delights when people desire to worship Him with all their hearts. No one wants to force their fellowship on others.

The Difference between Moses and the Children of Israel

Psalm 103:7 He (God) made known his ways unto Moses, his acts unto the children of Israel. Moses knew the ways of God, but the children of Israel only knew His acts. Psalm 95:10 Forty years long was I grieved with this generation, and said, it is a people that do err in their heart, and they have not known my ways. Let us learn the heartbeat of God. Let us enter his presence and worship him in spirit and in truth and learn God's ways. 2Corinthians 3:16-18 Nevertheless when it (the heart) shall turn to the Lord, the vail shall be taken away. Now the Lord is that Spirit and where the Spirit of the Lord is, there is liberty. But we all, with open face beholding as in a glass the glory of the Lord, are changed into the same image from glory to glory, even as by the Spirit of the Lord. As our worship is based upon his word, not merely our experiences we begin to act and talk just like him.

The New and Living Way

Hebrews 10:19-20 Having therefore brethren boldness to enter into the holiest by the blood of Jesus by a new and living way. In the Old Testament, the "holiest" was a place where only the high priest could enter. However, under the new covenant, the door to the holy place is open to all believers who will enter in. We enter in through the blood of Jesus Christ!

Matthew 27:50-51 Jesus, when he had cried again with a loud voice, yielded up the ghost. And, behold, the veil of the temple was rent in twain from the top to the bottom; and the earth did quake, and the rocks rent. According to Josephus the veil was about 4 inches thick and 60 feet high. It was so strong that horses were tied to it on either end and could not pull it apart. When the veil was torn God was saying I am not living there in longer I refuse to be separated from you. From now on I will make my home in you. Hebrews 9:8 The Holy Ghost this signifying, that the way into the holiest of all was not yet made manifest, while as the first tabernacle was yet standing. In order to establish the second, He had to get rid of the first.

Hebrews 8:6 But now hath he obtained a more excellent ministry, by how much also he is the mediator of a better covenant, which was established upon better promises. Within the Old Covenant they stayed away from his presence to live. Within the New Covenant we draw near to live.

Hindrances to Worship

These are not in any order and the list is not comprehensive, so you can add to it if you wish.

#1 Come to God with a Clean Conscience

Having our hearts sprinkled from an evil conscience. God does not want us to come to Him with sins of the soul. In other words, inward sins like jealousy, bitterness, and hatred. He wants us to be clean of every sin and our conscience to be pure.

#2 When You Stand Praying, Forgive

Many believers love to quote Mark 11:24-25 Therefore I say unto you, what things so ever ye desire, when ye pray, believe that ye receive them, and ye shall have them. And when ye stand praying, forgive; if ye have ought against any that your Father also which is in heaven may forgive you your trespasses.

Jesus was wise to warn us of the greatest hindrance to the prayer of faith, which is unforgiveness.

#3 A Lack of Knowledge

When we come into God's presence, we must come with a heart filled with faith. Faith comes from knowledge of the Word of God. A lack of knowledge will hinder us from genuinely enjoying worship. In the Old Testament, David brought the Ark of the Covenant into the nation of Israel and into Jerusalem with a lack of knowledge. He carried the ark improperly by carrying it on a cart when God had given instruction for rods to be run through the ark and for the priests to carry it on their shoulders. Because of a lack of knowledge as to how to carry the ark, a man ended up dying when he tried to steady the ark. Your lack of knowledge can affect innocent people around you. God will forgive us for the lack of knowledge, but the further we walk with Him, the more accountable He will expect us to be. God's desire is that we continue to grow in our knowledge of His Word. Often, people will try to separate worship from the study of God's Word, but they cannot be separated. Whenever you study God's Word, you are worshiping. The word "worship" means, "face to face kissing with God." We should not treat the study of God's Word lightly because again, it is a form of worship.

#4 Pride

1 Corinthians 1:29 The Word says no flesh should glory in his presence. It doesn't say that flesh cannot come into His presence; it says no flesh shall glory in His presence. Pride always lifts itself above others, as being better than others. God hates pride and the arrogant heart. He hates a haughty spirit. He loves a humble heart and promises to exalt the humble person in due time. Proverbs 8:13 The fear of the LORD is to hate evil pride, and arrogancy, and the evil way, and the froward mouth, do I hate. 1Corinthians 4:7 For who maketh thee to differ from another? And what hast thou that thou didst not receive? Now if thou didst receive it, why dost thou glory, as if thou hadst not received it? I stated earlier in this revelation I consider myself a gift, and so should you. I am a gift that can only be received by faith. As Kingdom Musicians thinking this way keeps you grounded, you are not offended by rejection, nor filled with pride because you are received. John 13:20 Verily, verily, I say unto you, He that

receiveth whomsoever I send receiveth me; and he that receiveth me receiveth him that sent me. Years ago, my wife and I we're invited to a Television Studio here in Atlanta, we were introduced to a Christian celebrity; she looked at us like we had leprosy. That is the attitude God hates.

#5 An Independent Attitude

John 15:5 I am the vine, ye are the branches. He that abideth in me, and I in him, the same bringeth forth much fruit for without me ye can do nothing. Jesus is the vine and we are the branches. Without the life that comes from the vine, the branches could not produce. We are totally dependent upon the vine. Without the Lord, we can do nothing. An independent attitude will keep us from truly worshiping God. The way to stay attached to the vine is by remaining in fellowship with God. When we begin to have an independent attitude, we cut ourselves off from the vine that feeds us. Stay in the word. Not only are we dependent on Him but we should be interdependent on one another. 1Corinthians 12:14-16 For the body is not one member, but many. If the foot shall say, Because I am not the hand, I am not of the body; is it therefore not of the body? And if the ear shall say, Because I am not the eye, I am not of the body; is it therefore not of the body?

#6 A Critical Attitude

We need to be removed from a critical attitude. The Word of God repeatedly warns against judging others. A critical attitude is really a manifestation of pride. When someone is critical, they are setting themselves up as a judge to look down on and speak evil of other people. The only person we have a right to judge is ourselves. The Bible tells us that we are to examine ourselves. But often, we spend time judging others than we do ourselves. Matthew 7:1-3 Judge not, that you be not judged. For with what judgment you judge, you shall be judged and with what measure you mete, it will be measured to you again. And why behold thou the mote that is in thy brother's eye, but consider not the beam that is in your own eye? Jesus is saying, "How dare you judge another person. How dare you criticize them when they have only a splinter in their eye, but you have a log in your eye! "By criticizing others, you have reaped back a good measured, pressed down, shaken together, and running over splinter! Whatever you sow, you will reap. That is why it is so important to sow love!

When you judge others, you are in worse condition than any sin they might be participating in. Romans 2:1 Therefore you are inexcusable, O man, whosoever you are that judges: for wherein you judge another, you condemn yourself; for you that judge do the same things. Over the years I have noticed in my own ministry times when the anointing was stronger than others. I have noticed that love and faith have a lot to do with experiencing a greater glory.

#7 Apathy

Apathy is laziness, lack of interest, enthusiasm, or concern.

Apathy will stop you and I from entering the goodness of God. Ministry is active. Ecclesiastes 10:18 By much slothfulness the building decays, and through idleness of the hands the house drops through. Be diligent to develop your fellowship and your call before the Lord.

#8 Impatience

Hebrews 6:12 That ye be not slothful, but followers of them who through faith and patience inherit the promises. James 1:4 But let patience have her perfect work, that you may be perfect and entire, wanting nothing. All these areas must be developed if personal and corporate worship is to mature.

#9 Legalism

Legalism is a subtle hindrance. By legalism I mean believing our works make us worthy to enter his presence. By legalism I mean our traditions making the word of God of no effect. Mark 7:13 Making the word of God of none effect through your tradition, which ye have delivered: and many such like things do ye.

#10 Worldliness

1 John 2:15 Love not the world, neither the things that are in the world. If any man love the world, the love of the Father is not in him. 2Timothy 4:10 For Demas hath forsaken me, having loved this present world, and is departed unto Thessalonica; Crescens to Galatia, Titus unto Dalmatia.

What you do is always a product of what you think. Your thoughts precede your actions. We cannot allow worldliness into our worship before the Father.

1 John 2:16 For all that is in the world, the lust of the flesh, and the lust of the eyes, and the pride of life, is not of the Father, but is of the world. We are inundated with the Spirit of the world on every side.

#11 Wrong Priorities

Giving God our left-over time, squeezing him into our schedule, instead of building our schedule around him.

Matthew 6:33 But seek first the kingdom of God and His righteousness, and all these things shall be added to you.

Exodus 20:3 You shall have no other gods before Me.

Matthew 4:89 Again, the devil took Him up on an exceedingly high mountain, and showed Him all the kingdoms of the world and their glory. And he said to Him, "All these things I will give You if You will fall down and worship me."

Chapter 5

THE NEED TO DRAW NEAR

There are times of great needs, or a love one is facing a serious challenge and we are tempted to focus on the problem. We must always remember Jesus is the answer. I do not mean in a religious sense; I mean we should look to him on purpose. Let me give you a few examples. If someone gets a headache do, they reach for the bible or the aspirin? If there's the need for money do they look to God or someone or some institution to borrow from? What is your initial reaction to adversity? You see many times we believe God in church but in everyday life we become our own lords. This is the life that worships; this is the life that draws its strength from him. Total dependence is what we need. Acknowledging him in all our ways allowing him to direct our path.

James 4:1-7 From whence come wars and fightings among you? Come they not hence, even of your lusts that war in your members? Ye lust, and have not: ye kill, and desire to have, and cannot obtain: ye fight and war, yet ye have not, because ye ask not. Ye ask, and receive not, because ye ask amiss, that ye may consume it upon your lusts. Ye adulterers and adulteresses know ye not that the friendship of the world is enmity with God? Whosoever therefore will be a friend of the world is the enemy of God. Do ye think that the scripture saith in vain, The spirit that dwelleth in us lusteth to envy? But he giveth more grace. Wherefore he saith, God resisteth the proud, but giveth grace unto the humble. Submit yourselves therefore to God. Resist the devil, and he will flee from you.

James says there are internal pressures if not handled properly will manifest in strife towards our love ones. There are desires that go unfulfilled and we can blame that on the ones closest to us. The pressure can cause separation from love ones and God. James says God will give grace to those who humble themselves or those who role the whole of their care on him. A parenthetical definition for grace in verse 6 in the *Amplified bible* is (the power of the Holy Spirit, to meet this evil tendency and all others fully). This is the reason people give out and give up; this is the reason for defeat in the life of an informed believer. There is the need to draw near and stay near. Remember the Lord told Martha that Mary had chosen that good part which shall not be taken away from her.

In my office as Pastor I have watched it over the years how the word is the first thing to go in the lives of some believers. It is substituted for TV entertainment or just being plain old lazy. I have watched people attempt to make major decisions without the word being first place and things end up disastrously. Yes, we have took work, we must cut the grass, we must take little Johnny to the ball game and yet in the final analysis only one thing is really needed.

I have noticed in my own life whenever I have been inconsistent it can be traced back to not spending time or not enough quality time in His presence. I remember where I was in my spiritual life when Keisha one of our daughters went to be with the Lord. There is no pressure like the pressure of losing a child and yet there is this grace that James talks about. The power of the Holy Spirit to meet this evil tendency and all others. In that case the pressure to give way to grief. I mean every pressure. Money, family it does not matter. Drawing near to Him and then making His face your home. His presence will strengthen you it will hold you up when life's pressures try to knock you down. I remember standing in front of our daughter her spirit already with the Father. I just drop to my knees and cried in tongues. But when I rose, I knew that the greater one lived in me I knew that to be absent from the body is to be present with Him.

His presence must be paramount in your life or there will be continual failure and weakness. There is a place in Him a place of dependency, where you are comfortable with letting him be boss. There is a place where weakness is turned to strength and inconsistency melts like snow when it gets hot. Remember James says you lust and have not you kill (he's making reference to hatred) and you cannot obtain you lust and war.

The Life That Worships

Drawing near for clean hands and a pure heart

James 4:8 Draw nigh to God, and he will draw nigh to you. Cleanse your hands, ye sinners; and purify your hearts, ye double minded. The ball is in your court it is your move, to get him involved in your affairs get involved with him. Make those needed changes he has been speaking to you about for months and some things for years. The children of Israel knew God's acts, but Moses knew his ways. Spending time with him, until you smell just like him. I remember once

I picked Miss Ella up at one of the boy's home she was in the kitchen around the food when she got in the car, she smelled just like what was being cooked. Drawing near being transformed by the fellowship you have with him daily. Growing from glory to glory while in his presence.

2Corinthians 7:1 Having therefore these promises, dearly beloved, let us cleanse ourselves from all filthiness of the flesh and spirit, perfecting holiness in the fear of God.

Contemporary English Version -My friends, God has made us these promises. So we should stay away from everything that keeps our bodies and spirits from being clean. We should honor God and try to be completely like him.

Easy To Read Version- Dear friends, we have these promises from God. So we should make ourselves pure—free from anything that makes our body or our soul unclean. Our respect for God should make us try to be completely holy in the way we live.

Our respect for him and our preoccupation with his face causes us to be just like him in our thoughts and actions. Get this and do not forget it, when you draw near to him, you are automatically resisting the devil.

Exodus 20:21 And the people stood afar off, and Moses drew near unto the thick darkness where God was. You can see this holy boldness in Moses' life and ministry. His fearless approach to God is recorded many times. We have been given a standing invitation to come boldly to the throne of grace in Hebrews 4:16.

The Need To Draw Near

Exodus 33:12-16 *New International Version*- Moses said to the Lord, "You have been telling me, 'Lead these people,' but you have not let me know whom you will send with me. You have said, 'I know you by name and you have found favor with me.' If you are pleased with me, teach me your ways so I may know you and continue to find favor with you. Remember that this nation is your people." The Lord replied, "My Presence will go with you, and I will give you rest." Then Moses said to him, "If your Presence does not go with us, do not send us up from here. How will anyone know that you are pleased with me and with your people unless you go with us? What else will distinguish me and your people from all the other people on the face of the earth?"

This is such an awesome passage let us chew on it some.

- Moses states that God's favor is tied to knowing his ways.

- Moses states I am not going without your presence (remember God did not live in them the way he lives in us).

- Moses states your presence will distinguish us from all the other people of the earth.

- Moses says your presence is your stamp of approval.

You can see that Moses was adamant about the presence of the Father God. It reminds me of what Paul said. 1Corinthians 15:10 But by the grace of God I am what I am and his grace which was bestowed upon me was not in vain; but I labored more abundantly than they all: yet not I, but the grace of God which was with me.

Matthew 11:28-30 Come unto me, all ye that labor and are heavy laden, and I will give you rest. Take my yoke upon you, and learn of me; for I am meek and lowly in heart: and ye shall find rest unto your souls. For my yoke is easy, and my burden is light.

In the Greek language the words give rest is one word it literally means I will rest (you). His presence brings with it rest. When you have the water, you have the wet when you have God's presence you have rest.

The Life That Worships

Easy To Read Version Come to me all of you who are tired from the heavy burden you have been forced to carry. I will give you rest. Accept my teaching. Learn from me. I am gentle and humble in spirit. And you will be able to get some rest. Yes, the teaching that I ask you to accept is easy. The load I give you to carry is light."

The Message Translation "Are you tired? Worn out? Burned out on religion? Come to me. Get away with me and you'll recover your life. I'll show you how to take a real rest. Walk with me and work with me—watch how I do it. Learn the unforced rhythms of grace. I won't lay anything heavy or ill-fitting on you. Keep company with me and you'll learn to live freely and lightly."

Drawing near for rest

Hebrews 4:9-11 There remaineth therefore a rest to the people of God. For he that is entered into his rest, he also hath ceased from his own works, as God *did* from his. Let us labor therefore to enter into that rest, lest any man fall after the same example of unbelief (the word means disobedience).

The word *rest* means the deeper rest that the Christian should enjoy; it represents a rest that closes the manifold forms of earthly preparation and work. Not an isolated Sabbath but a Sabbath life. The word labor means to make haste to be zealous or eager. You decide to do this. You like Mary choose the good part. I have said it before I will say it again this should be the foundation all our efforts.

A Greater Glory

Finding your place to walk in your grace is essential not only for effective ministry but a joy filled Christian life. To know every morning when you get up what the Father created you to be and do is fulfilling. In the ministry of worship all are not called to take the same approach, I notice that in my life and ministry I tend to lean more towards talking to the Father than talking about Him. Others on the other hand do a great job at the gate of Thanksgiving and in the court of Praise. I am not talking about tempo or style I am talking about position.

Many of the songs the Father has given me over the years are repetitive in lyrical arrangement because my grace is to promote face to face fellowship. I am comfortable with that and you should be also. We define the different graces upon our lives a little differently than the Father does. We call it black gospel, country gospel, rock gospel and so on. The Father calls it a grace, and an office and a gift.

Rom 12:3-6 For I say, through the grace given unto me, to every man that is among you, not to think *of himself* more highly than he ought to think; but to think soberly, according as God hath dealt to every man the measure of faith. For as we have many members in one body, and all members have not the same office: So we, *being* many, are one body in Christ, and every one members one of another. Having then gifts differing according to the grace that is given to us.

I remember in the early eighties I would follow hard after Larnell Harris in my music ministry to me he was and is the epitome of music ministry. Then as I begin to develop my own grace, I found that there were people who were following hard after me. Someone said imitation is the highest form of flattery.

Paul states that the measure of faith is for us to operate in the grace given to us. He even gives us an example, he said for I say through the grace given to me. Do you see that? He's saying, what I'm about to say I'm graced to say. Let me do the same thing, we need more of that. We need people to write more songs from the grace instead of what the current style is. I can see it happening more and more, songs birth out of fellowship and not solely writing ability. Again I say what I say through this grace upon my life.

Psalms 22:3 But thou *art* holy, *O thou* that inhabitest the praises of Israel. The praise that He lives in is spontaneous worship. He enjoys all praise but He lives in the spiritual song.

Tehillah teh-hil-law- to sing, to laud. A spontaneous new song. Singing from a melody in your heart by adding words to it. This refers to a special kind of singing it is singing unprepared, unrehearsed songs. It brings tremendous unity to the body of Christ.

Singing straight to God. Can move you into tehilah anytime. Singing it the second time would be ZAMAR. It is the praise that God inhabits (sits enthroned on).

The Life That Worships

Scripture: Psalms 22:3, 34:1, 40:3, 66:2, 2 Chronicles 20:22

Let us look at 2Chronicles 20:22 And when they began to sing and to praise, the LORD set ambushments against the children of Ammon, Moab, and mount Seir, which were come against Judah; and they were smitten.

This is spontaneous Worship this type of praise is the spiritual song in manifestation. This is the song that He lives in. I believe there should be Believers meetings where we give the Holy Spirit space to manifest as He wills. There is a greater glory by that I mean a deeper place of reverence and revelation in worship that we need to attain to.

I remember in the earlier days of this ministry I would worship all the time. I remember as time passed being cautioned by Him not to abandon that time of fellowship. I was going to visit a friend once and after praying in the Spirit I opened my mouth and begin to sing there was a time when I would fall before your face I time when I'd sing with a heart filled with grace and in those times I'd long for fellowship with you those times I long for those times.

Then after a moment of silence He began to sing to me (I mean through my vocal chords). There was a time when you would fall before my face a time when you'd sing with a heart filled with grace and in those times I'd long for fellowship with you those times I long for those times.

Tears of intimacy filled my eyes, as joy filled my heart to know that He longs for fellowship with me. To know that He desires my presence and that I am welcome before His face. Colossians 2:10 And ye are complete in him, which is the head of all principality and power. The exchange when we sang to each was such a blessing to me, but He reminded me He was just as blessed by my presence as I was His. Ephesians 1:23 Which is his body, the fulness of him that filleth all in all. Please don't miss that He is our fullness but we are His fullness.

This is part of the fight of faith. Satan is already defeated so this fight is a fight to remain attached to the Father.

John 15:5 I am the vine, ye *are* the branches: He that abideth in me, and I in him, the same bringeth forth much fruit: for without me ye can do nothing.

You understand that the same life that is in the vine is in the branches. All that He is He has made us. We worship Him with the revelation that we have His name and ability. 1Corithians 1:30 But of him are ye in Christ Jesus, who of God is made unto us wisdom, and righteousness, and sanctification, and redemption.

How To Stay Connected

To prepare for ministry Luke 4:1-2 And Jesus being full of the Holy Ghost returned from Jordan, and was led by the Spirit into the wilderness, Being forty days tempted of the devil. And in those days he did eat nothing: and when they were ended, he afterward hungered. Luke 4:14-15 And Jesus returned in the power of the Spirit into Galilee: and there went out a fame of him through all the region round about. And he taught in their synagogues, being glorified of all.

To get refilled after ministry Mark 6:30-32 And the apostles gathered themselves together unto Jesus, and told him all things, both what they had done, and what they had taught. And he said unto them, Come ye yourselves apart into a desert place, and rest a while: for there were many coming and going, and they had no leisure so much as to eat. And they departed into a desert place by ship privately.

To deal with grief Matthew 14:9 -13 And the king was sorry: nevertheless for the oath's sake, and them which sat with him at meat, he commanded it to be given her. And he sent, and beheaded John in the prison. And his head was brought in a charger, and given to the damsel: and she brought it to her mother. And his disciples came, and took up the body, and buried it, and went and told Jesus. When Jesus heard of it, he departed thence by ship into a desert place apart: and when the people had heard thereof, they followed him on foot out of the cities.

Before making an important decision Luke 6:12-13. And it came to pass in those days, that he went out into a mountain to pray, and continued all night in prayer to God. And when it was day, he called unto him his disciples: and of them he chose twelve, whom also he named apostles;

In a time of distress Luke 22:39-44 And he came out, and went, as he was wont, to the mount of Olives; and his disciples also followed him. And when he was at the place, he said unto them, Pray that ye enter not into temptation. And he was withdrawn from them about a stone's cast, and kneeled down, and prayed, Saying, Father, if thou be willing, remove this cup from me: nevertheless not my will, but thine, be done. And there appeared an angel unto him from heaven, strengthening him. And being in an agony he prayed more earnestly: and his sweat was as it were great drops of blood falling down to the ground.

Private communion with the Father Luke 5:16 And he withdrew himself into the wilderness, and prayed.

Prayer for Salvation And Baptism
in the Holy Spirit

Heavenly Father, I come to You in the name of Jesus. Your Word says, "Whosoever shall call on the name of the Lord shall be saved" (Acts 2:21) I am calling on You.. I pray and ask Jesus to come into my heartand be Lord over my life according to Romans 10:9-10 "That if thou shalt confess with thy mouth the Lord Jesus, and shalt believe in thine heart that God hath raised him from the dead, thou shalt be saved. For with the heart man believeth unto righteousness; and with the mouth confession is made unto salvation." I do that now. I confess that Jesus is Lord, and I believe in my heart that God raised Him from the dead. I repent of sin. I renounce it. I denounce the devil and everything he stands for. Jesus is my Lord.

I am now reborn! I am a christian, a child of Almighty God! I am saved! You also said in our Word, "If ye then, being evil, know how to give good gifts unto your children: HOW MUCH MORE shall your Heavenly Father give the Holy Spirit to them that ask Him?" (Luke 11:13). I'm also asking you to fill me with the Holy Spirit. Holy Spirit, rise up within as I praise God. I fully expect to speak with other tongues as You give me utterence (Acts 2:4). In Jesus Name. Amen!

Begin to praise God for filling you with the Holy Spirit. Speak those words and syllables you receive--not in your own language, but the language given to you by the Holy Spirit. You have to use your own voice. God will not force you to speak. From now on you will never be the same.

Find a good bible teaching church to aid in your spiritual growth. Fellowship is important to us as believers. Find your ministry and glorify God.

Make a habit to view Bible Answers and feed on other materials from our website and social media channels.

About The Author

Willie Browning is a pastor psalmist and author with over forty years of living what is being taught in The Life Worships. He comes from a rich heritage of faith his Father a Pastor and His Mother a teacher of the Word in the ministry.

He has travelled teaching praise and worship since the late eighties with an undeniable grace that comes from God. By precept and example the audience is shown how to live in the Father's presence.

He and his wife Ella pastor His Presence Church in Stockbridge Ga and he is studying for his degree at Anderson Theological Seminary.

Learn more about his worship ministry by visiting **lihpschoolofworship.org**